Neanderthal Culinary Traditions

René Vermandois

Published by R. Vermandois, 2023.

While every precaution has been taken in the preparation of this book, the publisher assumes no responsibility for errors or omissions, or for damages resulting from the use of the information contained herein.

NEANDERTHAL CULINARY TRADITIONS

First edition. October 23, 2023.

Copyright © 2023 René Vermandois.

ISBN: 979-8223771074

Written by René Vermandois.

Table of Contents

neanderthal-food

Neanderthal Culinary Traditions

Preface: Sophisticated Culture That Extended Beyond Tool-Making and Hunting

In recent years, researchers have made intriguing discoveries regarding Neanderthal culinary traditions, shedding light on the development of human diets as we know them today.

To truly understand the impact of Neanderthal culinary practices, it is essential to delve into their dietary habits. Through the analysis of fossil remains, scientists have uncovered valuable clues about the Neanderthal menu. These early humans were opportunistic eaters, heavily reliant on the available resources in their respective environments. While their primary diet consisted of animal meat, including large game like bison and deer, Neanderthals also supplemented their meals with various wild plants, such as tubers, berries, and nuts.

One significant aspect of Neanderthal culinary traditions is their mastery of fire. The control and use of fire were transformative milestones in human history, enabling our ancestors to enhance the flavors and nutritional value of their meals. Neanderthals were highly skilled at creating and maintaining fires, and evidence suggests that they used controlled flames to cook their food. By roasting meat over an open fire, they not only made it easier to chew and digest but also reduced the risk of parasites and other pathogens.

Beyond the act of cooking itself, Neanderthals demonstrated a level of culinary innovation that continues to surprise scholars to this day. Excavations at Neanderthal sites have revealed evidence of ancient hearths lined with herbs and spices, leading researchers to believe that these early humans possessed a rudimentary knowledge of seasoning. It is fascinating to consider that they may have used aromatic plants to add flavor and complexity to their dishes, much like modern culinary practices.

Moreover, recent studies of dental calculus, the hardened plaque found on teeth, have provided even deeper insights into Neanderthal dietary habits. By examining the microscopic plant particles trapped in dental calculus, scientists have identified remnants of cooked starches from plants like barley and cattails. This discovery suggests that Neanderthals not only enjoyed roasted meats but also experimented with plant-based foods, perhaps boiling or steaming them to create nourishing and appetizing meals.

While these culinary practices eventually faded into history with the extinction of the Neanderthals, their legacy lives on within modern human diets. Traces of Neanderthal genetic influence can still be found in the DNA of present-day humans, particularly in populations with Eurasian ancestry. This genetic legacy not only shaped our physical characteristics but also influenced our dietary preferences, as certain populations have inherited

Chapter 1: Introduction to Neanderthals

Neanderthals, our ancient cousins, have long captivated the imaginations of scientists and historians alike. These mysterious beings, who roamed the Earth some 400,000 to 40,000 years ago, left behind a rich tapestry of evidence that gives us valuable insights into their lives and their place in human evolution. In this chapter, we will delve into the world of Neanderthals, exploring their characteristics and setting the stage for an exciting journey into their culinary traditions.

When Neanderthals were first discovered in the mid-19th century in the Neander Valley of Germany, they were often portrayed as primitive and inferior to modern humans. However, subsequent scientific research has debunked these misconceptions and revealed that Neanderthals were highly adapted and skilled beings who successfully inhabited diverse environments.

One of the most striking characteristics of Neanderthals was their physical appearance. They had a muscular and robust build, with a stocky body and shorter limbs compared to modern humans. Their distinctive features also included a large nose, prominent brow ridges, and a receding forehead. These adaptations allowed them to thrive in harsh, cold climates, such as those of Ice Age Europe.

Neanderthals were not mere brutes; they possessed intelligence and creativity. Recent studies have revealed that they had a brain size comparable to that of modern humans and possessed the ability for language. While we may never recover the direct evidence of their spoken words, the discovery of a gene associated with speech and language in Neanderthal DNA suggests that they possessed a complex system of communication.

As skilled hunters and gatherers, Neanderthals utilized a wide range of tools and technology to survive and thrive in their environments. Their toolkit included handaxes, spear points, and scrapers, which were all crafted with great precision. This indicates their advanced cognitive ability and their ability to plan and execute complex tasks.

In addition to their hunting expertise, Neanderthals also had an extensive knowledge of plants and their medicinal properties. Evidence from archaeological sites has revealed the use of diverse plant species, some of which possessed antimicrobial and pain-relieving properties. This suggests that Neanderthals had a sophisticated understanding of medicinal plants and their applications.

Understanding Neanderthals in the context of human evolution is crucial to gaining a comprehensive view of our own species. Genetic studies have shown that Neanderthals and modern humans share a common ancestry, with interbreeding occurring between the two groups in the past. In fact, it is estimated that individuals of non-African descent today carry about 1-2% of Neanderthal DNA, highlighting our deep connection to these ancient beings.

Now that we have laid the groundwork for exploring Neanderthal culinary traditions, we can begin to unravel the mysteries of their diet and culinary practices. By examining the remnants left behind at archaeological sites, such as food remains and cooking tools, we can piece together a fascinating story of what and how Neanderthals ate.

Chapter 2: Unveiling the Neanderthal Diet

Investigating the evidence and methods used to uncover the Neanderthal diet involves delving into a world that existed thousands of years ago. This journey requires us to rely on the remnants left behind, including fossilized remains, ancient DNA, and dental calculus. By piecing together these various clues, we can get a glimpse into the culinary traditions of our enigmatic ancestors.

Fossilized remains play a crucial role in our understanding of the Neanderthal diet. As archaeologists unearth skeletal remains from different sites, they meticulously analyze the bones to determine what they can reveal about the prehistoric diet. By examining the isotopic composition of the bones, researchers can discern whether Neanderthals mainly consumed meat or if they incorporated plant resources into their diet as well. The ratios of stable isotopes of carbon and nitrogen in the bone collagen can shed light on the primary sources of food. A higher ratio of 15N to 14N suggests an increased consumption of meat, while a lower ratio indicates a more plant-based diet.

Analyzing ancient DNA has also proven instrumental in uncovering the Neanderthal diet. Scientists have extracted genetic material from ancient Neanderthal bones and used advanced sequencing techniques to decode their genomes. Within these genetic sequences, researchers search for specific genes related to metabolism or digestion. These genes provide insights into the types of food that Neanderthals were genetically adapted to consume. For instance, the presence of genes responsible for breaking down starch suggests a diet that included starchy plant foods.

Further supplementing our understanding are the discoveries made through the analysis of dental calculus. Dental calculus, commonly known as dental plaque, is the hardened deposit that forms on teeth. This calcified material not only preserves microscopic traces of food particles, but it also captures information about the oral microbiome. Through advanced techniques such as proteomics and ancient DNA analysis, scientists can identify the specific food sources, including plant materials and animal proteins, that once passed through the mouths of Neanderthals. By examining dental calculus from different individuals across various sites, we can begin to piece together the broader picture of the Neanderthal diet.

Combining these different sources of evidence, archaeologists have started to unravel the complex dietary habits of Neanderthals. It appears that their diet was much more diverse than previously believed. While these ancient hominins were undoubtedly skilled hunters and scavengers, their diet was not confined solely to meat. Instead, they incorporated a variety of plant resources into their meals. Analyses of dental calculus have revealed remnants of plant foods, such as tubers, seeds, and even medicinal plants. This suggests a surprisingly sophisticated understanding of local flora and the ability to exploit different food sources.

However, it is important to note that the Neanderthal diet was not uniform across all populations and regions. Differences in available resources and environmental conditions influenced their dietary choices. Neanderthals adapted to various habitats, from cold and forested regions to more open landscapes. These adaptations likely influenced the availability and composition of their diet. In colder areas, where meat may have been more readily available, a higher consumption of animal protein might have been observed.

As we delve deeper into the archaeology of appetite, the tangible pieces of evidence are painting a fascinating picture of Neanderthal culinary traditions. The analysis of fossilized remains, ancient DNA, and dental calculus has provided invaluable insights into their dietary habits. However, many questions still remain unanswered. What cooking techniques did they employ? How did they process and preserve their food? These tantalizing mysteries await exploration in the second half of this chapter, where we will further unravel the Neanderthal diet and take a closer look at the cooking methods and cultural significance of their meals. Stay tuned for the next installment of our journey into the intriguing world of our ancient ancestors.

As we delve deeper into the archaeology of appetite, the tangible pieces of evidence are painting a fascinating picture of Neanderthal culinary traditions. The analysis of fossilized remains, ancient DNA, and dental calculus has provided invaluable insights into their dietary habits. However, many questions still remain unanswered. What cooking techniques did they employ? How did they process and preserve their food? These tantalizing mysteries await exploration in the second half of this chapter, where we will further unravel the Neanderthal diet and take a closer look at the cooking methods and cultural significance of their meals.

One significant aspect of Neanderthal culinary practices that researchers have been able to uncover is the evidence of cooking. The ability to control fire and cook food is a defining characteristic of human evolution, and recent studies have provided evidence that Neanderthals were indeed capable of utilizing fire for cooking purposes. By analyzing the remains of ancient hearths and fire pits, archaeologists have discovered charred food remains, bone fragments, and even evidence of cooking utensils.

These findings suggest that Neanderthals were not simply consuming raw meat or foraging on uncooked plants. Cooking their food not only made it more palatable and easier to digest, but it also had other potential benefits. Cooking likely had a profound impact on the nutritional quality of their meals by making certain nutrients more accessible and reducing the risk of bacterial or parasitic infections.

To gain a better understanding of how Neanderthals processed and preserved their food, researchers have turned to the microscopic examination of stone tools. These tools reveal evidence of butchering techniques, such as cut marks on bones, which indicate the removal of meat from carcasses. Additionally, the presence of scraping tools suggests that Neanderthals were skilled at skinning animals to obtain valuable hides for clothing and shelter.

Another intriguing element of their culinary practices relates to the cultural significance of food. Food has always played a pivotal role in human societies, serving not only as a means of sustenance but also as a way to establish social bonds, express cultural identity, and convey symbolic meanings. Just as we have cultural and traditional foods today, Neanderthals likely had their own unique culinary traditions that were passed down from one generation to the next.

While we cannot fully comprehend the symbolic meanings attached to their meals, some evidence points to a potential social dimension. For example, the discovery of burnt bones and discarded food remains at communal fire pits suggests that Neanderthals may have gathered together to share meals. These communal activities may have fostered cooperation, communication, and a sense of community among group members.

Furthermore, the inclusion of various plant resources in their diet hints at a level of dietary diversity that goes beyond mere sustenance. Certain plants may have been chosen for their medicinal properties, contributing to the overall well-being and health of Neanderthal communities. The utilization of these plants, alongside their hunting and gathering activities, demonstrates a deep connection to the natural world and an intimate knowledge of their environment.

It is important to note that our understanding of Neanderthal culinary traditions is constantly evolving as new archaeological discoveries and scientific techniques emerge. With each new excavation, researchers uncover more pieces of the enigmatic puzzle that is the Neanderthal diet. By meticulously analyzing and interpreting these ancient remains, we are slowly gaining deeper insights into the lives and habits of our ancient ancestors.

In conclusion, the archaeological investigation of the Neanderthal diet has shed light on their sophisticated culinary traditions. Fossilized remains, ancient DNA analysis, and the study of dental calculus have revealed a more diverse diet than previously believed, incorporating both meat and plant resources. Furthermore, the evidence of cooking, butchering techniques, and communal dining practices suggests an advanced level of food processing, preservation, and socialization. As we continue to unravel the mysteries surrounding Neanderthal culinary traditions, we gain a better understanding of our own human origins and the deep-rooted relationship between food, culture, and evolution.

Chapter 3: Hunting Techniques and Meat Consumption

Neanderthals, often depicted as primitive and subhuman, were, in fact, highly skilled hunters. Their hunting practices and the consumption and preparation of meat in their diet were integral to their survival and development as a species. In this chapter, we will explore the fascinating world of Neanderthal hunting techniques and shed light on their culinary traditions.

The hunting practices of Neanderthals were primarily focused on securing food for their communities. They employed a range of techniques to capture animals, which varied depending on the landscape and prey availability. One of the most common methods utilized by Neanderthals was ambush hunting. They would patiently wait in concealed positions, using their knowledge of animal behavior and natural surroundings to predict their prey's movements.

To increase their chances of success, Neanderthals developed an impressive array of tools for hunting. One of their most iconic implements was the spear. These spears were skillfully crafted from wood, bone, or antler, and often coupled with sharp stone points. This combination allowed for greater penetrating force, ensuring a higher success rate in bringing down their prey.

In addition to spears, Neanderthals also utilized thrusting spears and throwing spears, which allowed them to attack from a distance. These hunting tools were a testament to their ingenuity and resourcefulness, demonstrating a sophisticated understanding of physics and the mechanics required for effective hunting.

Meat consumption played a vital role in the Neanderthal diet, providing essential nutrients and sustaining their energy levels. The consumption of meat not only satisfied their appetites but also allowed for the growth and development of their communities. Recent archaeological evidence suggests that Neanderthals were skilled at butchering animals, utilizing various techniques to extract the most meat from their kills.

Upon successfully capturing their prey, Neanderthals would carry out extensive butchering procedures. They would carefully remove the skin, separate the different cuts of meat, and even exploit the bones for marrow extraction. The bones themselves were also valuable tools for Neanderthal communities. They were used to fashion various implements, including needles and scrapers, which further enhanced their ability to process and utilize the resources available to them.

It is important to note that the Neanderthal culinary traditions extended beyond the mere consumption of meat. They exhibited a level of sophistication in their cooking techniques, utilizing fire for both cooking and food preservation. Fire not only provided warmth and protection but also transformed the taste and texture of their meals. Neanderthals would skillfully roast, boil, or smoke their meat, adding flavors and improving its digestibility.

Moreover, cooking allowed for the transformation of tough and sinewy meats into tender and palatable dishes. The controlled application of heat and the addition of herbs, spices, and other natural ingredients greatly enhanced the flavor profiles of their meals. This development in culinary techniques not only showcased their mastery of fire but also demonstrated a level of innovation in harnessing the elements to alter food properties.

As we delve deeper into the intricacies of Neanderthal culinary traditions, it becomes evident that their hunting practices and meat consumption were not merely primal instincts but sophisticated adaptations for survival. The strategic use of tools, the intricate process of butchery, and the culinary advancements they made all contributed to their ability to secure sustenance, thrive, and ultimately shape their communities.

Hunting was not a solitary endeavor for Neanderthals; it was a communal activity that fostered cooperation and strengthened social bonds. The distribution of tasks among members of the group was crucial for a successful hunt. It is believed that differentiation of gender roles could have played a role in hunting practices. While men were likely the primary hunters, women and children also contributed by gathering plant-based food sources or participating in smaller-scale hunting activities.

The social dynamics of Neanderthal hunting can be inferred from the archaeological record. Evidence suggests that the division of labor, exchanges of knowledge, and cooperation within the group were vital. When a successful hunt occurred, the distribution and sharing of meat within the community were critical for both sustenance and social cohesion. This practice created a sense of reciprocity and ensured that everyone in the group received a fair share of the resources.

Meat consumption had profound cultural and social implications for Neanderthal communities. It served not only as a source of nutrition but also as a means of social differentiation and display. The availability and quality of meat could signify an individual's social status within the group. Those who had access to more desirable cuts of meat or specialized hunting tools may have held higher positions within the social hierarchy.

Furthermore, the sharing of meat played a role in the formation and maintenance of alliances between different groups. Meat may have been used as a form of currency or as a gift to establish relationships and trade networks. This suggests that the social and cultural significance of meat extended beyond its nutritional value, highlighting its role in fostering connections and cooperation between Neanderthal communities.

The Neanderthals' interaction with other species was not limited to hunting. They likely engaged with animals in various ways, including scavenging. Evidence from archaeological sites indicates that Neanderthals had the capability to exploit animal carcasses left behind by other predators. This scavenging behavior allowed them to obtain additional sources of meat and utilize resources that would have otherwise gone to waste.

Moreover, the Neanderthals' relationship with animals extended beyond practicality. The presence of animal remains in burial sites suggests a reverence for these creatures and the acknowledgment of their importance in Neanderthal culture and belief systems. These animals, both in life and death, held a significant place in the lives of Neanderthals, fostering a deep connection between the two.

As our understanding of Neanderthal culinary traditions continues to evolve, it becomes clear that their hunting practices and meat consumption went beyond mere sustenance. They were interwoven with social, cultural, and spiritual aspects, shaping the fabric of Neanderthal communities. The knowledge and skills developed in hunting, butchery, and culinary techniques formed a cornerstone of their survival, prosperity, and ability to adapt to diverse environments.

Neanderthals' hunting practices and meat consumption were multifaceted endeavors that impacted not only their physical well-being but also their social structures, cultural practices, and interactions with the natural world. As we uncover more archaeological discoveries and unravel the complexities of their culinary traditions, we gain a deeper appreciation for the adaptability and sophistication of these remarkable beings who once roamed the earth.

Chapter 4: Gathering and Foraging

Neanderthals, often portrayed as brutish and primitive, were actually skilled gatherers and foragers. Just like modern humans, these ancient hominins relied on their environment to sustain themselves, indulging in a wide range of food sources, including plants, nuts, and other edible resources. Through an examination of their consumption habits, we gain a fascinating insight into the culinary traditions of these early humans.

In contrast to popular belief, Neanderthals did not solely rely on hunting large game. While hunting played a significant role in their diet, the gathering and foraging activities of Neanderthals should not be overlooked. Research has revealed that plants formed a notable proportion of their food intake. By studying the dental calculus, plaque residue found on Neanderthal teeth, scientists have identified remnants of various plant materials. This includes traces of berries, tubers, and even pollen from flowers, shedding light on their foraging habits.

One of the primary plant food sources in the Neanderthal diet was nuts. From acorns to hazelnuts, they actively sought out these nutrient-rich morsels. The abundance of nut remains found at archaeological sites suggests that Neanderthals had an intricate knowledge of their environment, knowing where to locate and exploit these valuable resources. Utilizing stone tools to crack open shells, they unlocked an additional source of sustenance that would have sustained them throughout the year.

However, it is noteworthy that the gathering and foraging practices of Neanderthals were not solely limited to plants and nuts. They were opportunistic eaters, adapting to the available resources in their surroundings. This included consuming various invertebrates such as insects, shellfish, and even small mammals. The evidence for these dietary choices lies in the presence of insect remains, mollusk shells, and small mammal bones found at archaeological sites.

Foraging for plant resources required Neanderthals to have a deep understanding of their surroundings. They had to identify which plants were edible, which parts were suitable for consumption, and when they were at their most nutritious. Ethnographic studies of modern-day foragers shed further light on the potential methods utilized by Neanderthals, such as observation, experimentation, and knowledge handed down through generations.

Furthermore, the geographical locations inhabited by Neanderthals influenced the variety of vegetation they utilized. In regions with a diverse plant life, their diet would have consisted of a wide array of edible plants. Analysis of dental calculus samples has shown the presence of pollen from different plants, revealing a rich botanical tapestry that contributed to their culinary traditions. Understanding the regional variations in Neanderthal diets provides valuable insights into their adaptation to different environments across Europe and western Asia.

The gathering and foraging activities of Neanderthals not only allowed them to meet their nutritional needs but also showcased their cognitive abilities. Adaptability, resourcefulness, and a nuanced knowledge of their environment were vital for their survival. By diversifying their food sources, Neanderthals demonstrated a deep connection with their surroundings, transcending the stereotype of them being solely brutish hunters.

As we delve deeper into the intriguing world of Neanderthal culinary traditions, it becomes apparent that they were far more sophisticated than previously thought. Their gathering and foraging practices shed light on their complex relationship with the environment and their ability to sustain themselves through diverse food sources. Join us in the next part of this chapter as we explore the fascinating world of Neanderthal hunting strategies and its impact on their culinary traditions. Brace yourself for a journey into the hunting prowess of these ancient hominins, as we unveil their fascinating techniques and surprising discoveries.

Hunting played a significant role in the Neanderthal's food procurement strategy. Their ability to successfully hunt large game animals, such as mammoths, woolly rhinoceroses, bison, and deer, provided them with a substantial source of protein and fat. Evidence of hunting can be found in the presence of animal bones with cut marks and fractures, as well as the remains of bone tools used for butchering and processing carcasses.

Neanderthals employed several techniques and weapons to bring down their prey. Spearing was a common method, with thrusting spears used to pierce vital organs. The successful use of these weapons required strength, skill, and coordination. Neanderthals were also skilled at ambush hunting, utilizing natural features to hide and surprise their prey.

The archaeological record also reveals the use of hunting traps by Neanderthals. Pitfall traps, where large game animals would fall into a concealed pit, were an effective way to capture prey. The presence of bones and other remains in these pits suggests that Neanderthals may have used them repeatedly, indicating a level of planning and strategizing in their hunting practices.

Another intriguing aspect of Neanderthal hunting was the utilization of social strategies. Hunting in groups would have offered several advantages, such as increased chances of success, cooperative hunting techniques, and the ability to share resources. This social aspect of hunting likely played a crucial role in the survival and prosperity of Neanderthal communities.

While the consumption of large game animals was undoubtedly important for the Neanderthals' survival, they also targeted smaller prey. The remains of small mammals, birds, and fish have been found in archaeological sites, suggesting that Neanderthals were skilled hunters of a variety of game. These smaller animals would have provided a more readily accessible and reliable food source, especially during times when large game was scarce.

Interestingly, evidence also indicates that Neanderthals were capable of hunting with a level of selectivity. For example, they may have targeted specific age groups or sizes of animals, utilizing their knowledge of animal behavior and ecology. This selectivity demonstrates their ability to adapt their hunting strategies to ensure the sustainability of their resources and maintain a diverse diet.

Neanderthals also made use of the resources provided by their environment in innovative ways. They exploited the bones, antlers, and skins of hunted animals, transforming them into tools, clothing, and shelter. The ingenuity and resourcefulness displayed in their ability to repurpose animal remains showcase the intricate relationship between hunting, gathering, and survival for these ancient hominins.

In conclusion, the culinary traditions of Neanderthals were shaped by their gathering, foraging, and hunting practices. Far from being solely brutish hunters, they showcased adaptability, resourcefulness, and a deep understanding of their environment. Through a combination of foraged plants, nuts, small mammals, shellfish, and their hunting prowess, Neanderthals were able to sustain themselves and thrive across a wide range of environments.

As we continue to uncover the complexities of Neanderthal culinary traditions, we gain a better understanding of their cultural and cognitive abilities. The archaeological record offers a glimpse into their remarkable strategies for procuring and preparing food, revealing a sophisticated society that was intimately connected to the natural world.

Join us in the next chapter as we explore the fascinating world of Neanderthal cooking techniques and the transformative role fire played in their culinary traditions. Embark on this captivating journey into the realm of ancient cooking practices, as we unravel the mysteries of the archaeological evidence left behind by these incredible hominins.

Chapter 5: Food Processing and Cooking Techniques

Neanderthals, our ancient ancestors, may not have had access to the modern conveniences that we enjoy today, but they were masters at adapting to their environment and utilizing the resources available to them. In order to survive and thrive, Neanderthals had to develop innovative methods of processing and cooking their food. This chapter delves into the ways Neanderthals processed their food, such as grinding, pounding, and cooking, and explores the impact on their culinary traditions and nutrition.

Food processing was a vital part of Neanderthal culture. By processing their food, they were able to break down tough plant materials and make them more palatable and easier to digest. One of the main techniques Neanderthals used was grinding. Archaeological evidence suggests that they would grind various plant materials, such as seeds, grains, and nuts, using stone tools. This process not only made the food more accessible but also released nutrients that would have otherwise remained locked within the tough outer shells.

Pounding was another common method employed by Neanderthals in food processing. They would use heavy stone tools to pound animal bones, extracting every bit of nutrient-rich marrow. The bones would also be cracked open to access the valuable protein and fat reserves. By harnessing pounding techniques, Neanderthals were able to extract maximum sustenance from their prey, making every part of the animal useful for their survival.

Perhaps one of the most significant advancements in Neanderthal culinary traditions was the discovery of cooking techniques. The ability to cook food had far-reaching implications for their health, cultural development, and even their cognitive abilities. Cooking not only improved the flavor of food but also made it more easily digestible, reducing the energy required for their bodies to process and extract nutrients.

By applying heat to their food, Neanderthals were able to break down complex proteins, rendering them more easily assimilated by the body. This increased the efficiency of their digestion and absorption processes, providing them with a greater nutritional yield from their meals. Furthermore, cooking also played a crucial role in reducing the risk of foodborne illnesses, as the heat destroyed harmful pathogens present in raw meats and other food items.

Cooking was not limited to meat alone; Neanderthals also experimented with cooking plant materials. Heat allowed them to soften tough fibers and break down potentially toxic compounds, making these plants safer for consumption. As a result, Neanderthals incorporated a wider range of plant-based foods into their diets, contributing to their overall dietary diversity and nutritional intake.

The shift towards more processed and cooked food had profound effects on Neanderthals' culinary traditions. As they became more proficient in food processing and cooking techniques, they were able to manipulate flavors, textures, and even create new culinary traditions that were passed down through generations. This development marked a significant shift in their culture and social interactions, as meals became not just a means of sustenance but also a way to gather, celebrate, and express their communal identity.

Moreover, the adoption of cooking techniques had implications beyond culinary advancements. The increased availability of nutrient-rich food sources provided Neanderthals with a greater energy surplus. This surplus, in turn, fueled their physical strength, cognitive development, and the ability to adapt to their ever-changing environments. The mastery of food processing and cooking may have been a pivotal factor in the survival and success of the Neanderthal population.

In conclusion, the archaeological evidence unequivocally demonstrates that Neanderthals were highly skilled in processing and cooking their food. Through techniques such as grinding, pounding, and cooking, they were able to unlock the nutritional potential of diverse food sources and develop a rich culinary tradition. These advancements not only enhanced their health and well-being but also fostered social connections and cultural developments within their communities. Join us in the second half of this chapter as we explore the fascinating world of Neanderthal cuisine and delve deeper into the impacts of their culinary traditions on their daily lives and survival.

The Neanderthals' mastery of food processing and cooking techniques not only revolutionized their diets but also had profound implications for their daily lives and survival. In this section, we will delve deeper into the impacts of their culinary traditions and explore the fascinating world of Neanderthal cuisine.

The adoption of more sophisticated food processing techniques enabled Neanderthals to manipulate flavors, textures, and even develop new culinary traditions. As they became more proficient in grinding and pounding, they were able to extract maximum sustenance from every part of their prey. This ensured that no part of the animal went to waste and contributed to their overall dietary diversity.

Moreover, the discovery of cooking techniques had far-reaching implications for Neanderthal society. Cooking not only improved the flavor and palatability of their food but also made it more easily digestible, reducing the energy required for their bodies to process and extract nutrients. This increased their nutritional yield from meals, providing them with a greater energy surplus.

The surplus energy derived from their processed and cooked food sources played a vital role in fueling Neanderthals' physical strength and cognitive development. With a more nutrient-rich diet, they were able to sustain higher levels of physical activity, contributing to their survival in challenging environments. Additionally, the increased availability of energy-rich foods may have supported the development of larger brains and enhanced cognitive abilities, allowing Neanderthals to adapt to their ever-changing surroundings.

The shift towards more processed and cooked food had implications beyond culinary advancements. Meals became a focal point for social gatherings, celebrations, and the expression of communal identity. The act of cooking and sharing meals created bonds within Neanderthal communities and fostered social connections. As culinary traditions were passed down through generations, they became an essential part of Neanderthal culture.

Furthermore, the adoption of cooking techniques also played a crucial role in reducing the risk of foodborne illnesses. The application of heat during cooking destroyed harmful pathogens present in raw meats and other food items, ensuring the safety of their meals. This newfound ability to minimize the threat of foodborne diseases may have had positive effects on Neanderthal health and well-being, leading to longer lifespans and reduced mortality rates.

Neanderthals did not limit their culinary explorations to meat alone; they also experimented with cooking various plant materials. By applying heat, Neanderthals were able to soften tough fibers and break down potentially toxic compounds present in certain plants. This made these plants safer for consumption and expanded their dietary options. The incorporation of a wider range of plant-based foods contributed to their overall dietary diversity and nutritional intake.

The mastery of food processing and cooking techniques was undoubtedly a pivotal factor in the survival and success of Neanderthals as a species. It allowed them to adapt to their environment, utilize available resources to their fullest potential, and overcome nutritional challenges. By unlocking the nutritional potential of diverse food sources, Neanderthals were able to sustain themselves in a wide range of habitats, enabling them to colonize different regions.

In conclusion, the archaeological evidence highlights the remarkable culinary skills of Neanderthals in processing and cooking their food. The techniques of grinding, pounding, and cooking unlocked the nutritional potential of various food sources, fostered cultural developments within their communities, and played a significant role in their survival. Join us in the next chapter as we further explore the fascinating world of Neanderthal cuisine, uncover additional insights from archaeological findings, and delve into the links between their culinary traditions and their cultural and social lives.

Chapter 6: Neanderthal Food Storage and Preservation

As we delve into the fascinating world of Neanderthal culinary traditions, one cannot help but wonder about their resourcefulness and ingenuity when it came to storing and preserving food. Neanderthals, much like their modern human counterparts, recognized the importance of food storage to ensure survival during times of scarcity or when resources were not readily available. In this chapter, we will explore the methods used by Neanderthals to achieve this, including food caching techniques and the remarkable use of natural refrigeration.

Food caching, or the practice of stockpiling food in hidden or protected locations, was a crucial strategy employed by Neanderthals. It allowed them to gather and preserve food supplies, ensuring a steady source of sustenance throughout the year. But how exactly did they cache their food? Archaeological evidence suggests that Neanderthals utilized several strategies, each suited to different types of food and environmental conditions.

One technique observed in various Neanderthal sites involves the use of pits for storing food. These pits were dug into the ground, lined with plant materials or animal hides, and then filled with provisions. The design of these storage pits effectively protected the food from scavengers and helped regulate temperature and humidity, promoting preservation. By utilizing such storage facilities, Neanderthals were able to prolong the shelf life of perishable items, such as meat and fruits, allowing them to be consumed long after the animal or plant had perished.

Another ingenious method employed by Neanderthals involved the use of natural refrigeration. During colder months or in areas with frigid temperatures, they took advantage of ice and snow to preserve food. Neanderthals would construct storage areas, often within natural ice caves or snow-covered crevices, to take advantage of the chilly conditions. These icy environments acted as natural refrigerators, maintaining a consistently low temperature that prevented spoilage and preserved food over extended periods. Within these makeshift cold storage spaces, Neanderthals could store meat, fish, and even provisions like nuts and berries, allowing them to be consumed during times when food was scarce.

Archaeological excavations have also revealed evidence of advanced food preservation techniques utilized by Neanderthals. For instance, the discovery of partially desiccated meat indicates their ability to dehydrate and preserve their food. Neanderthals may have achieved this through various means, such as air drying or smoking. By removing moisture from the meat, they eliminated the conditions that promote bacterial growth, thus extending its longevity. Furthermore, the smoking process also imparted a distinct flavor to the food, enhancing its palatability and potentially contributing to their culinary traditions.

The successful storage and preservation of food required knowledge of the local environment, resource availability, and the natural behaviors of different plants and animals. Neanderthals were keen observers of their surroundings and learned through trial and error the ideal conditions for preserving different food items. This knowledge was likely passed down through generations, creating a rich and complex culinary tradition that adapted to the diverse landscapes they inhabited.

As we uncover the secrets of Neanderthal food storage and preservation, we gain insights into their resourcefulness and adaptability. These early humans understood the importance of safeguarding precious food resources and developed innovative methods to overcome challenges. But what other surprises await us in the second half of this chapter? How did Neanderthals ensure the longevity of their stored food? Join us as we delve deeper into their culinary practices and unravel the mysteries of Neanderthal ingenuity and survival.

One technique employed by Neanderthals to preserve their food involved the process of fermentation. Fermentation is a natural metabolic process that breaks down carbohydrates in the absence of oxygen, resulting in the production of alcohol, lactic acid, or other organic compounds. Neanderthals utilized fermentation as a preservation method for various food items, including fruits, vegetables, and even grains.

Archaeological evidence indicates that Neanderthals intentionally stored fruits, such as wild berries or plums, in containers or pits. These fruits would undergo fermentation over time, effectively preserving them for consumption during periods when fresh supplies were scarce. The fermentation process not only extended the shelf life of these fruits but also altered their taste and texture, providing Neanderthals with a range of flavor profiles.

Another intriguing aspect of Neanderthal food storage and preservation lies in their use of natural preservatives. Neanderthals had a profound understanding of the properties of certain plants, such as herbs and spices, that possessed antimicrobial or antioxidant properties. They would incorporate these natural preservatives into their food storage practices to prevent spoilage and enhance the flavor of their meals.

For example, Neanderthals may have used plants with antimicrobial properties, such as juniper berries or thyme, to rub onto meat before storage. These plants contain compounds that inhibit the growth of bacteria, effectively safeguarding the meat from spoiling. Additionally, the use of plants rich in antioxidants, like rosemary or sage, could have prevented the oxidation of fats, thus preserving the quality and taste of stored meat over extended periods.

Furthermore, Neanderthals displayed great ingenuity in developing techniques for food preservation that involved dehydration. Removing moisture from food inhibits bacterial growth and prevents spoilage, allowing them to store various perishable items for future consumption.

One notable method utilized by Neanderthals was air drying. They would hang meat or fish in well-ventilated areas, taking advantage of natural airflow to facilitate dehydration. By exposing the meat or fish to the air, moisture evaporated, effectively preserving the food and making it safe for consumption during times of scarcity.

In addition to air drying, Neanderthals possibly employed smoking to enhance food preservation. Smoking not only dehydrates the food but also introduces antimicrobial compounds found in the smoke, further inhibiting bacterial growth. This method would have been particularly advantageous for preserving larger quantities of meat and extending its longevity.

The ability to cure and preserve meat not only served as a source of nutrition but also contributed to the development of Neanderthal culture and community. Preserved meat would have allowed for the provision of food during gatherings or events, promoting social cohesion, and reinforcing social bonds within their groups.

Equally intriguing is the evidence of Neanderthals' use of trapped air as a method of food preservation. In certain circumstances, Neanderthals would carefully remove air from containers, such as animal bladders or intestines, before sealing them. Trapped air within these containers acted as a barrier against bacterial contamination, facilitating the preservation of food items stored within them.

As we piece together the complexities of Neanderthal food storage and preservation, it becomes evident that their culinary practices extended far beyond mere sustenance. These methods allowed Neanderthals to adapt to various environmental conditions, ensuring a steady food supply during both abundance and scarcity.

Moreover, the preservation techniques employed by Neanderthals were not limited to meat or animal products alone. They also demonstrated an understanding of the seasons and the cyclic availability of certain plant resources. By preserving fruits, nuts, and grains, Neanderthals were able to enjoy a diverse diet year-round, regardless of the shifts in resource availability.

The accomplishments of Neanderthals in food storage and preservation are a testament to their resourcefulness and adaptability as a species. Through trial and error, they honed their knowledge of the natural world, observed the behaviors of different plants and animals, and developed innovative techniques to overcome the challenges they faced in acquiring and preserving food.

With the close of this chapter, we are left with a deep appreciation for the ingenuity and resourcefulness of Neanderthal culinary traditions. Their ability to store and preserve food offered them not only sustenance but also the means to navigate a rapidly changing world.

Chapter 7: Regional Variations in Neanderthal Diet

The study of Neanderthals has always fascinated historians, archaeologists, and anthropologists alike. Their existence, which spanned over 200,000 years, provides invaluable insights into our prehistoric past. One of the most intriguing aspects of Neanderthal life is their culinary traditions, which were shaped by the regional variations and availability of food sources around them.

To truly understand the Neanderthal diet, we must delve into the archaeological evidence left behind. The remains of their cooking hearths, bone tools, and waste piles offer a glimpse into their food preferences and the techniques they employed in meal preparation. By examining these remnants, researchers have been able to reconstruct their diets and shed light on the regional variations that existed within the Neanderthal population.

In the lush forests of Europe, where Neanderthals thrived for thousands of years, their diet was largely influenced by the abundance of plant resources. Studies have shown that they relied heavily on berries, nuts, and roots, supplementing their plant-based diet with the occasional wild game. The discovery of charred seeds and plant matter near their hearths suggests that Neanderthals were proficient in cooking these resources, unlocking their nutritional value by applying heat.

Moving eastwards, into the expansive steppes of Central Asia, the Neanderthal diet took a shift towards a more carnivorous approach. The harsh environment and scarcity of vegetation meant that Neanderthals had to adapt to survive. They became skilled hunters, focusing on large herbivores such as mammoths and bison. These massive creatures provided them with not only sustenance but also raw materials for clothing and shelter.

Interestingly, in the arid plains of Africa, a distinct Neanderthal culinary tradition emerged. Fossil evidence suggests that they had a strong reliance on fish and shellfish, taking advantage of the rich coastal resources available to them. Their use of mollusk shells as tools and the presence of fish remains near their campsites provide compelling proof of their aquatic diet. This adaptation to a maritime environment showcases the remarkable adaptability and resourcefulness of these early humans.

The varied regional diets of Neanderthals were not simply a result of their surrounding environments. Their culinary traditions were also influenced by the cultural exchanges that occurred when different groups interacted. Archaeological sites that show a mix of food remains from various regions suggest that Neanderthals engaged in trade or shared knowledge about food sources. These interactions may have led to the adoption of new foods and cooking techniques, further diversifying their diet.

As we uncover more information about Neanderthal culinary traditions, it becomes increasingly evident that their diet was not only dictated by environmental factors but was also shaped by their innate curiosity and adaptability. The Neanderthals were not the primitive brutes often depicted in popular culture; they were resourceful and intelligent beings who thrived in a ever-changing world.

Understanding the regional variations in the Neanderthal diet is a crucial piece in unraveling the mysteries of our ancient past. By examining the archaeological evidence and piecing together these dietary patterns, we gain valuable insights into the interplay between humans and their environment. This knowledge allows us to appreciate the incredible resilience and evolutionary adaptability of our distant ancestors.

The Neanderthals, our ancient human ancestors, inhabited diverse regions across the world, each with its own unique environment and available food sources. In this second half of Chapter 7: Regional Variations in Neanderthal Diet, we will explore in more depth the culinary traditions of Neanderthals in Europe, Central Asia, and Africa. By delving into the archaeological evidence, we can gain a deeper understanding of how these early humans adapted to their surroundings and utilized the resources at their disposal.

Europe, with its lush forests and diverse plant life, provided an ideal habitat for the Neanderthals. The abundant plant resources such as berries, nuts, and roots formed a significant part of their diet. However, it was not solely a plant-based diet as they also incorporated wild game into their meals. Excavations near their cooking hearths have revealed charred seeds and plant matter, suggesting that the Neanderthals skillfully cooked these resources to enhance their nutritional value. The ability to utilize fire for cooking unlocked new possibilities for the Neanderthals, allowing them to extract vital nutrients and make their mark on culinary history.

Moving eastwards into the vast steppes of Central Asia, the Neanderthals faced a starkly different environment. The scarcity of vegetation in these arid plains forced them to adapt to survive. Here, their diet shifted towards a more carnivorous approach with a focus on hunting large herbivores such as mammoths and bison. These majestic creatures not only provided sustenance but also offered raw materials for clothing and shelter. The Neanderthals' resourcefulness and hunting skills were crucial to their survival in this challenging landscape.

In the arid plains of Africa, the Neanderthals developed a distinct culinary tradition. Fossil evidence indicates that they heavily relied on fish and shellfish as a primary food source, taking advantage of the rich coastal resources available to them. The presence of mollusk shells as tools and the discovery of fish remains near their campsites provides compelling proof of their aquatic diet. The adaptability demonstrated by the Neanderthals in utilizing coastal resources showcases their remarkable resilience and ingenuity.

While the unique regional diets of Neanderthals can be attributed to the environmental factors of each region, there is evidence to suggest that cultural exchanges among different groups also played a significant role. Archaeological sites with a mixture of food remains from various regions indicate trade or the sharing of knowledge about food sources. These interactions likely led to the adoption of new foods and cooking techniques, further diversifying their diet. The Neanderthals' culinary traditions were not stagnant but evolved through a dynamic process of exchange and innovation.

As we piece together the archaeological evidence, it becomes increasingly clear that the Neanderthals were far from the primitive brutes often portrayed in popular culture. They were resourceful and intelligent beings who adapted to their ever-changing world. The diverse diets they maintained were a testament to their ability to navigate the challenges posed by their environments and exploit the available resources to their advantage.

Understanding the regional variations in the Neanderthal diet offers valuable insights into our ancient past. Through these dietary patterns, we gain a deeper understanding of the interplay between humans and their environment throughout history. The Neanderthals' ability to adapt and survive in diverse landscapes highlights the remarkable resilience and evolutionary adaptability of our distant ancestors.

As we conclude our exploration of the regional variations in Neanderthal culinary traditions, we come to appreciate the profound impact their diets had in shaping their cultures and their ability to adapt to a changing world. The archaeological evidence left behind by these early humans provides us with a window into our prehistoric past, offering valuable lessons about our own connection to food and the environment. By studying the archaeological record and recognizing the innovation and adaptability of our ancestors, we can better understand our own journey as humans and the intricate relationship between ourselves and the world around us.

In closing, we extend our gratitude to the tireless researchers and archaeologists who spend their lives unearthing the remnants of the past and piecing together the mysteries of our ancient origins. It is through their dedication and discoveries that we continue to deepen our understanding of our shared history and the incredible diversity of human experience across time and place. *Neanderthal Culinary Traditions* invites us to reassess our perception of the Neanderthals and celebrate their rich cultural heritage – a testament to their resilience, adaptability, and ingenuity.

Chapter 8: Neanderthal Feasting and Ritual Foods

———

Food, throughout history, has not only been a means of sustenance but also a powerful social and cultural tool. It has played a key role in bringing people together, fostering bonds, and solidifying community structures. Neanderthals, our ancient human relatives, were no strangers to the significance of food in their own lives. In this chapter, we delve into the intriguing social aspects of Neanderthal food consumption, exploring their feasting practices, communal meals, and the role of food in rituals and gatherings.

Feasting, in particular, was an important social event for Neanderthals. These gatherings were often marked by abundance, as evidenced by the large quantities of bones and artifacts found at some archaeological sites. It appears that Neanderthals engaged in feasting during specific times of the year, using it as a way to strengthen social connections and display their resourcefulness and social standing within the group.

At feasts, Neanderthals would come together to share food and engage in various activities. The communal aspect of these meals fostered a sense of belonging and camaraderie within the group. Sharing food was not only a way to ensure everyone's survival but also a way to forge and maintain social bonds. The act of communal dining created a shared experience that may have helped Neanderthals build trust and cooperation, enabling them to navigate their challenging environment more effectively.

The types of foods consumed during these feasts varied depending on the availability of resources and seasonal factors. Neanderthals were skilled hunters and gatherers, adapting their diet to the ever-changing environment. Animal remains found at archaeological sites reveal a wide range of prey, including large mammals like bison, deer, and horses. These animals would have provided an abundant source of meat, while nuts, berries, and other plant-based resources supplemented their diet.

While feasting was undoubtedly a significant part of Neanderthal social dynamics, food also played a role in their rituals and gatherings. Archaeological evidence suggests that Neanderthals had rituals associated with food, which may have included ceremonial practices and beliefs surrounding the hunt, fertility, and the cycle of life. The careful placement of specific animal remains in certain areas, such as caves, suggests that these offerings held symbolic meanings and were part of a larger ritualistic framework.

Furthermore, the prevalence of communal activities related to food preparation suggests that Neanderthals engaged in collective efforts during these rituals and gatherings. The act of preparing and sharing meals together would have solidified social bonds and heightened emotional connections within the group. Food was not merely a physical necessity but also a gateway to the spiritual and social realms, an integral part of Neanderthal culture and identity.

As we continue to uncover more about Neanderthal culinary traditions, it becomes increasingly clear that the social aspects of food consumption played a crucial role in their lives. Feasting and communal meals provided opportunities for socialization, cooperation, and the formation of social hierarchies. Food held symbolic significance in their rituals and gatherings, connecting them to larger spiritual and cultural realms.

This exploration into Neanderthal feasting and ritual foods merely scratches the surface of their complex social dynamics. In the second half of this chapter, we will delve deeper into the cultural significance of Neanderthal culinary traditions, examining the role of food in religious practices, the symbolism attached to specific food items, and the ways in which these practices imparted a sense of identity and belonging within the Neanderthal community.

But for now, let us pause and reflect on the rich tapestry of Neanderthal social life that unfolds through their relationship with food. The remnants of these feasts and rituals continue to captivate archaeologists and historians alike, offering us a glimpse into the vibrant communal life and intricate cultural practices of our enigmatic ancient relatives.Neanderthals, our ancient human relatives, left behind a rich archaeological record that allows us to explore their unique culinary traditions and gain insights into their social dynamics. In the second half of this chapter, we delve deeper into the cultural significance of Neanderthal food consumption, examining the role of food in religious practices, the symbolism attached to specific food items, and the ways in which these practices imparted a sense of identity and belonging within the Neanderthal community.

Religious practices among the Neanderthals were closely intertwined with food. Rituals associated with hunting, fertility, and the cycle of life played a significant role in their spiritual beliefs. Some archaeological findings suggest that specific animals held symbolic meanings and were used in ceremonial settings.

The careful placement of animal remains, such as the skulls or antlers of a great beast, in specific areas like caves or natural formations, indicates that these offerings were part of a larger ritualistic framework. The Neanderthals likely sought to establish a connection with the spiritual realm, seeking favor or guidance from the powerful forces they believed governed their world.

But it wasn't just the physical remains of animals that held symbolic importance. Neanderthals also attached cultural significance to certain food items. For example, the discovery of charred pine nuts in hearths and settlements suggests that these nuts were not merely a dietary staple.

They may have been imbued with symbolic meaning, perhaps representing fertility or abundance.

In addition to their religious practices, Neanderthals engaged in communal activities related to food preparation. These collective efforts fostered social bonds and heightened emotional connections within the group. The act of gathering and preparing meals together created a shared experience, reinforcing a sense of belonging and cooperation.

Food preparation techniques also varied depending on the availability of resources and regional factors. Neanderthals displayed an impressive adaptability and resourcefulness when it came to culinary practices. We see evidence of this in the diverse range of tools and techniques used for processing and cooking food.

Stone tools, such as scrapers and knives, were employed to butcher and prepare animal carcasses. The remains of charred bones and plant material suggest that Neanderthals were adept at cooking their food over open fires. This not only made the food more palatable and easier to digest but also likely had hygienic benefits.

Beyond the practical aspects of food preparation, the sharing of meals fostered a sense of community and cooperation. It provided an opportunity for individuals to contribute to the sustenance of the group and solidify their social standing within the community. Neanderthals likely had a sophisticated understanding of reciprocity, and these communal meals may have served as a way to reciprocate social favors and strengthen social bonds.

Moreover, the act of sharing food was an essential component of social hierarchies within Neanderthal communities. The distribution of food resources could reflect the social status of individuals or families. Those who contributed more to the group, either through hunting or gathering, may have enjoyed higher prestige and influence within the community.

As we delve deeper into the complex social dynamics of Neanderthal culinary traditions, it becomes clear that food served as a tool for socialization, cooperation, and the formation of social hierarchies. Ritualistic practices tied to food consumption strengthened ties to the spiritual realm, reinforcing cultural identities and beliefs.

The remnants of Neanderthal feasts and rituals continue to captivate archaeologists and historians. Through their intricate relationship with food, we can decipher the vibrant communal life and rich cultural practices of our enigmatic ancient relatives. The study of Neanderthal culinary traditions provides us with important insights into the social lives, beliefs, and cultural practices of one of our closest human relatives.

As we conclude our exploration into the archaeological remnants of Neanderthal feasting and ritual foods, let us remember the profound significance of food in the human experience. From the prehistoric gatherings of our ancient ancestors to the shared meals of modern societies, food continues to enhance our social bonds and shape our cultural identities. By understanding the past, we gain a deeper appreciation for the role of food in our own lives and the enduring power of communal dining in fostering connections and building communities.

Chapter 9: Comparing Neanderthal and Homo sapiens Culinary Practices

Introduction:

Food has always been an essential part of human existence. Throughout history, our culinary practices have evolved and adapted, reflecting our unique cultural backgrounds and environmental circumstances. The study of Neanderthal culinary traditions provides us with valuable insights into the dietary habits and social customs of our ancient relatives. By comparing these practices with those of Homo sapiens, we can gain a deeper understanding of our shared history. In this chapter, we will explore the contrasts between Neanderthal and Homo sapiens culinary traditions, examining similarities and differences in food procurement, processing, and social customs.

Food Procurement:

For both Neanderthals and Homo sapiens, procuring food was a fundamental task for survival. However, the strategies employed by each group differed significantly. Neanderthals relied heavily on hunting large game, such as mammoths and bison, as their primary source of sustenance. Their robust physiques and unique hunting techniques, such as thrusting spears at close range, allowed them to successfully take down formidable prey.

In contrast, Homo sapiens exhibited a more diverse approach to food procurement. While hunting was still a vital part of their diet, they also incorporated gathering and fishing into their culinary practices. This wider range of food sources allowed Homo sapiens to adapt to various environments, ensuring a more stable food supply.

Food Processing:

Once food was secured, the processing techniques utilized by Neanderthals and Homo sapiens revealed interesting disparities. Neanderthals were proficient at simple but effective processing methods. They would often butcher large animals on the spot, utilizing every part to the fullest extent. This resourcefulness allowed them to minimize waste and make efficient use of their prey.

In contrast, Homo sapiens exhibited more elaborate and varied food-processing techniques. They utilized tools such as mortars and pestles to grind grains or nuts, enabling them to create flour or paste-like substances. They also employed techniques like smoking and drying to preserve food, extending its shelf life. This level of sophistication in food processing not only enhanced the visual appeal and taste of their meals but also allowed for experimentation and culinary innovation.

Social Customs:

Food has always played a significant role in shaping social customs and fostering human connections. Neanderthals, with their close-knit social groups, likely had a communal approach to dining. Sharing meals could have been a means of strengthening social bonds and reinforcing group cohesion. Evidence of communal food consumption can be seen from the presence of common hearths and food remains found at Neanderthal sites.

Homo sapiens, on the other hand, seemed to have developed more complex social dynamics around food. They began to exhibit signs of mealtime rituals and the sharing of special meals during gatherings or ceremonies. The emergence of symbolic art and decorations on food containers suggests that Homo sapiens attached cultural meanings to food, further highlighting their evolving social customs.

While Neanderthals primarily relied on hunting large game for sustenance, Homo sapiens exhibited a more diverse approach to food procurement. In addition to hunting, they incorporated gathering and fishing into their culinary practices, allowing them to adapt to various environments and ensuring a more stable food supply. The ability to gather a wide range of plant-based foods, such as fruits, nuts, tubers, and seeds, provided Homo sapiens with nutritional diversity.

Archeological evidence suggests that Homo sapiens were skilled gatherers, utilizing tools like digging sticks to extract roots and tubers from the ground. The gathering of wild fruits and nuts allowed them to supplement their diet with essential vitamins and minerals. Furthermore, the use of fishing nets, traps, and spears enabled Homo sapiens to capture freshwater and marine resources, expanding their food options.

Conclusion:

In comparing the culinary practices of Neanderthals and Homo sapiens, it becomes evident that both groups had distinct approaches to food procurement, processing, and social customs. Neanderthals relied heavily on hunting large game, while Homo sapiens diversified their food sources through gathering and fishing. When it came to food processing, Neanderthals showcased practical efficiency, whereas Homo sapiens exhibited more sophisticated techniques that allowed for culinary innovation. Socially, Neanderthals had a communal approach to dining, while Homo sapiens developed more complex social dynamics, attaching cultural significance to food and engaging in symbolic rituals.

By understanding the culinary traditions of our ancient relatives, we gain invaluable insights into our shared history and the diverse ways in which our ancestors adapted to their environments. Exploring the archaeology of appetite allows us to appreciate the rich tapestry of human experience and deepens our understanding of the complexities of our own culinary practices today. As we continue to unearth new discoveries and piece together these ancient food traditions, the study of Neanderthal and Homo sapiens culinary practices will continue to contribute to our understanding of human evolution.

Chapter 10: The Legacy of Neanderthal Culinary Traditions

The Neanderthals, ancient hominids that roamed the Earth thousands of years ago, have long fascinated archaeologists and scientists. Known for their robust physique and close genetic relationship to modern humans, these early humans possessed a sophisticated culture that extended beyond tool-making and hunting. In recent years, researchers have unearthed intriguing evidence suggesting that Neanderthals had their own culinary traditions, which left an indelible mark on the development of human diets as we know them today.

To understand the impact of Neanderthal culinary practices, we must first delve into their dietary habits. By analyzing fossil remains, scientists have uncovered valuable clues about the Neanderthal menu. These early humans were opportunistic eaters, relying heavily on the available resources in their respective environments. While their primary diet consisted of animal meat, including large game such as bison and deer, Neanderthals also supplemented their meals with an assortment of wild plants, including tubers, berries, and nuts.

One significant aspect of Neanderthal culinary traditions is their mastery of fire. The control and use of fire was a transformative milestone in human history that enabled our ancestors to enhance the flavors and nutritional value of their meals. Neanderthals were adept at creating and maintaining fires, and evidence suggests that they used these controlled flames to cook their food. By roasting meat over the open fire, they not only made it easier to chew and digest but also reduced the risk of parasites and other pathogens.

Beyond the straightforward act of cooking, Neanderthals also exhibited a level of culinary innovation that surprises scholars to this day. Excavations at Neanderthal sites have exposed evidence of ancient hearths lined with herbs and spices, leading researchers to believe that these early humans possessed a rudimentary knowledge of seasoning. It is fascinating to consider that they may have used aromatic plants to add flavor and complexity to their dishes, much like we do in modern culinary practices.

Moreover, recent studies of dental calculus, the hardened plaque found on teeth, have revealed even deeper insights into Neanderthal dietary habits. By examining the microscopic plant particles trapped in dental calculus, scientists have identified remnants of cooked starches from plants like barley and cattails. This discovery suggests that Neanderthals not only enjoyed roasted meats but also experimented with plant-based foods, perhaps boiling or steaming them to create nourishing and appetizing meals.

While these culinary practices of the Neanderthals eventually faded into history with their extinction, their legacy endures within modern human diets. In fact, traces of Neanderthal genetic influence can still be found in the DNA of present-day humans, particularly in populations with Eurasian ancestry. This genetic legacy not only shaped our physical characteristics but also influenced our dietary preferences, as certain populations have inherited an increased ability to digest certain food groups, such as meat and fat.

The impact of Neanderthal culinary traditions on modern human diets extends beyond genetics. The knowledge and skills passed down through generations have undoubtedly influenced the development and diversification of global cuisines. Techniques such as roasting, grazing on a variety of plant foods, and utilizing herbs and spices all have their roots in the practices of our ancient ancestors. As we savor the flavors and textures of our favorite dishes, we are unknowingly perpetuating the traditions of those who came before us.

In the second half of this chapter, we will delve deeper into the specific ways in which Neanderthal culinary practices have influenced modern human diets. From the incorporation of fire as a cooking tool to the utilization of plants for both nourishment and flavor, we will explore the intricate web of interconnectedness between our food traditions and those of our Neanderthal ancestors. Join us as we uncover the hidden history that lies within our contemporary culinary experiences. As we continue our exploration into the legacy of Neanderthal culinary traditions, it becomes increasingly evident that their influence on modern human diets is both profound and multifaceted. From the mastery of fire to the incorporation of plant-based foods, the interplay between our ancestors' culinary practices and our own is a rich tapestry that spans thousands of years.

Fire has long been recognized as one of the most significant advancements in human history, revolutionizing not only our ability to cook but also our food preferences and nutritional intake. The Neanderthals were no strangers to this transformative tool, adept at creating and maintaining fires to enhance their meals. The controlled use of fire provided numerous benefits, allowing for improved meat tenderness and digestion while reducing the risks associated with consuming raw or undercooked meats. This ingenious culinary innovation laid the foundation for our subsequent culinary traditions, influencing techniques such as grilling, baking, and smoking that are still prevalent today.

Beyond the mere act of cooking, the Neanderthals also exhibited a remarkable level of culinary innovation and sophistication. Excavations at their ancient sites have revealed evidence of hearths lined with herbs and spices, highlighting their rudimentary knowledge of seasoning.

These aromatic plants likely added complexity and depth of flavor to their dishes, much like the herbs and spices we commonly employ in modern cuisine. The use of seasonings not only enhanced the sensory experience of their meals but also showcased an early understanding of the culinary arts.

We can further uncover the Neanderthals' culinary repertoire through the analysis of dental calculus. By examining the microscopic plant particles trapped in the hardened plaque on their teeth, scientists have discovered remnants of cooked starches from plants like barley and cattails. This revelation suggests that Neanderthals not only relied on roasted meats but also experimented with plant-based foods, employing various cooking methods such as boiling or steaming to create nourishing and appetizing meals. This early exploration of an omnivorous diet, incorporating both animal and plant-based resources, laid the foundations for the diverse cuisines we enjoy today.

The impact of Neanderthal culinary traditions extends far beyond their dietary preferences and practices. Our genetic legacy, intertwined with that of these ancient hominids, has influenced our own ability to digest certain foods. Traces of Neanderthal genetic influence can still be found in the DNA of present-day humans, particularly in populations with Eurasian ancestry. This genetic legacy has shaped our physical characteristics, including a heightened ability to tolerate and process certain food groups, such as meat and fat. It is through these genetic adaptations that we can trace our ability to relish in the flavors derived from animal-based indulgences.

As we reflect on the enduring legacy of Neanderthal culinary traditions, it becomes evident that their contributions to our modern food traditions are vast and varied. Techniques such as grilling, roasting, and seasoning with herbs and spices, which were once mastered by our ancient ancestors, continue to form the bedrock of global cuisines.

Furthermore, the incorporation of a diverse range of plant-based foods into our diets echoes the early experimentation and utilization of such resources by the Neanderthals.

In conclusion, the archaeological evidence and genetic legacy left by the Neanderthals provide fascinating insights into their culinary practices and the lasting impact on our own food traditions. The mastery of fire, the utilization of seasonings, and the incorporation of plant-based resources all serve as a testament to their ingenuity and culinary innovation. As we savor the flavors and textures of our favorite dishes, we pay homage to the Neanderthals and honor the ancient roots that have shaped our contemporary culinary experiences. Join us in the subsequent chapters as we delve into more specific examples of Neanderthal culinary practices and their indelible mark on the diverse cuisines of the world.

For Further Reading

Adler, D. S., Barton, C. M., Collard, M., & Stringer, C. (2006). The shortfall of the Middle–to-Upper Paleolithic transition in the Iberian Peninsula. In Neanderthals and Modern Humans in the European Landscape of the Last Glaciation (pp. 89-114). McDonald Institute for Archaeological Research.

Bar-Yosef, O., & David, J. (2013). Cooking time and cooking temperature analysis in the Paleolithic. Current Anthropology, 54(S8), S373-S382.

Binford, L. R. (1968). Post-Pleistocene adaptations. In New Perspectives in Archaeology (pp. 313-341). Aldine Publishing Company.

Bocquet-Appel, J. P., & Demars, P. Y. (2000). Neanderthal contraction and modern human colonization of Europe. Antiquity, 74(286), 544-552.

Bower, J. R. F. (2018). When hominins flexed their muscles. Journal of Archaeological Method and Theory, 25(1), 287-305.

Bräuer, G., & Roksandic, M. (2019). Neanderthal biology and culture: perspectives on their origin and dispersal. Evolutionary Anthropology: Issues, News, and Reviews, 28(6), 266-268.

A., Brothwell, D., Copeland, L., ... & Thomas-Oates, J. (2015). Neanderthal medics? Evidence for food, cooking, and medicinal plants entrapped in dental calculus. Naturwissenschaften, 102(3-4), 42.

Cullen, H. (2015). Modern human-Neanderthal interbreeding: A tale of two species. PaleoAnthropology, 2015, 358-374.

Fiorenza, L., Benazzi, S., & Kullmer, O. (2011). Tooth wear and dentoalveolar remodeling are key factors of morphological variability in the Neanderthal mandible. PLoS ONE, 6(9), e26552.

Fu, Q., Posth, C., Hajdinjak, M., Petr, M., Mallick, S., Fernandes, D., ... & Bergström, A. (2016). The genetic history of Ice Age Europe. Nature, 534(7606), 200-205.

Hardy, K., Buckley, S., Collins, M. J., Estalrrich,

Hardy, K., Radini, A., Buckley, S., Blasco, R., Copeland, L., Burjachs, F., ... & Rosas, A. (2021). Neanderthal medics? Evidence for food, cooking, and medicinal plants entrapped in dental calculus from the Late Upper Paleolithic site of Cova Foradà. Quaternary International, 574, 80-99.

Henry, A. G., Brooks, A. S., & Piperno, D. R. (2014). Plant foods and the dietary ecology of Neanderthals and early modern humans. Journal of Human Evolution, 69, 44-54.

Higham, T., Douka, K., Wood, R., Ramsey, C. B., Brock, F., Basell, L., ... & Bergman, C. (2014). The timing and spatiotemporal patterning of Neanderthal disappearance. Nature, 512(7514), 306-309.

Hublin, J. J. (2009). The origin of Neanderthals. Proceedings of the National Academy of Sciences, 106(38), 16022-16027.

Lalueza-Fox, C., Rosas, A., Estalrrich, A., Gigli, E., Campos, P. F., García-Tabernero, A., ... & Willerslev, E. (2011). Genetic evidence for patrilocal mating behavior among Neanderthal groups. Proceedings of the National Academy of Sciences, 108(1), 250-253.

Lalueza-Fox, C., Rosas, A., Estalrrich, A., Gigli, E., Campos, P. F., García-Tabernero, A., ... & Willerslev, E. (2012). Cultural cannibalism as a paleoeconomic system in the European Pleistocene. Current Anthropology, 53(4), 436-452.

Mellars, P. A. (2006). A new radiocarbon revolution and the dispersal of modern humans

cross Eurasia. Antiquity, 80(310), 905-921.

Mithen, S., & Reed, K. (2002). Neanderthals mastered fire. Nature, 419(6909), 24-25.

Niven, L. (2015). Neanderthals and modern humans: an ecological and evolutionary perspective. Cambridge University Press.

Nowell, A., & Horstwood, M. (2017). A methodology for differentiating between single and multi-event depositional histories in caves with examples from Cova Gran (Spain) and Roche-Cotard (France). Journal of Archaeological Science, 79, 55-68.

Ortega, J., & Villa, P. (2009). Neanderthals and modern humans: the role of fire, clothing, and meat-eating. Quaternary Science Reviews, 28(25-26), 2995-3014.

Paijmans, J. L., Barlow, A., & Rabeder, G. (2017). Genetic diversity and population structure of cave bears (Ursus spelaeus) from eastern Europe. Journal of Quaternary Science, 32(1), 50-61.

Rozzi, R., & Massone, M. (2017). The taxonomic question: neanderthal taxonomy as seen from the comparative perspective. Quaternary International, 433, 271-277.

Smith, T. M., Tafforeau, P., Reid, D. J., Grün, R., Eggins, S., Boutakiout, M., ... & Hublin, J. J. (2007). Earliest evidence of modern human life history in North African early Homo sapiens. Proceedings of the National Academy of Sciences, 104(15), 6128-6133.

Spikins, P., Wright, B. J., Sam, D., & Scott, A. (2020). Human evolution and the appetite for meat. Cambridge Archaeological Journal, 30(2), 163-181.

Stringer, C., & Galway-Witham, J. (2017). On the origin of our species. Nature, 546(7657), 212-214.

Toussaint, M., Štrkalj, M., & Scott, A. (2019). When did Homo sapins migrate out of Africa? A review of the fossil and genetic evidence. Journal of Human Evolution, 128, 1-15.

Trinkaus, E. (2007). European early modern humans and the fate of the Neandertals. Proceedings of the National Academy of Sciences, 104(18), 7367-7372.

Trinkaus, E., Ruff, C. B., Brothwell, D., Stringer, C., & Zilhão, J. (2012). Late pleistocene human mandibles from the England-Scotland border: the influence of geography on early human dispersal. Journal of Human Evolution, 62(1), 89-103.

Verna, C., d'Errico, F., & Zilhão, J. (2012). The origin of blade production in the Levant as a result of environmental constraints. Journal of Archaeological Science, 39(4), 1352-1364.

Wang, C. Y., & Wintle, A. G. (2010). Radiometric geochronology and chronology of the last millennium. Quaternary Science Reviews, 29(5-6), 563-580.

Wolpoff, M. H., & Caspari, R. (1996). Race and human evolution: A fatal attraction. Simon and Schuster.

Zilhão, J., Davis, S. J., Duarte, C., Soares, A. M., Steier, P., Wild, E. M., & Mateus, J. (2010). Pego do Diabo (Loures, Portugal): dating the emergence of anatomical modernity in Westernmost Eurasia. PLoS ONE, 5(1), e8880.

Also by René Vermandois

Neanderthal Culinary Traditions
Skies of Destiny: Analyzing the Influence of Planetary Interpretations
in Medieval Europe and Islamic Golden Age
The Unofficial Kate Bush Self Help Book Satisfying Yearning,
Overcoming Obstacles Through Song Lyrics

www.ingramcontent.com/pod-product-compliance
Lightning Source LLC
Chambersburg PA
CBHW052235150726
48002CB00003B/1440